MORE EASY OBJECT TALKS
FOR TEACHING CHILDREN

by
Virginia Ann Van Seters

art by Richard Briggs

STANDARD
PUBLISHING
Cincinnati, Ohio

Dedicated to
the memory of
George T. Light,
the minister who saw in me
what I couldn't see.

Scripture quoted from the *International Children's Bible, New Century Version*, copyright © 1986, 1988 by Word Publishing, Dallas, Texas 75039. Used by permission.

ISBN 0-7847-0005-2

The Standard Publishing Company, Cincinnati, Ohio
A division of Standex International Corporation
Printed in the United States of America
00 99 98 97 96 95 94   5 4 3 2 1

Contents

Foreword

Miss Van Seters has done another excellent job in this her fifth volume of object talks in eight years. Her first four books, *22 Object Talks for Children's Worship, 26 Object Talks for Children's Worship, 26 More Object Talks for Children's Worship,* and *Easy Object Talks for Teaching Children,* all used a sound theological approach and provided practical and helpful directions. This latest contribution is no exception.

A fine Bible scholar and experienced children's leader, the author has prepared and used these talks, and now offers them to ministers and teachers.

Having spent 55 years in religious education as a seminary professor, Minister of Education, and supply pastor, I commend Miss Van Seters for her very original contributions to an important ministry.

Dr. John K. Durst

Introduction

These talks are presented here with complete instructions for delivery and any necessary recommendations for universal adaptation. They are written exactly as delivered, by a lay person, to show that, where more feasible, someone other than the minister can give them. All instructions are given in parentheses.

1

No Room in the Inn

(NOTE: This talk could be saved for Christmas.)

While Joseph and Mary were in Bethlehem, the time came for her to have the baby. She gave birth to her first son. There were no rooms left in the inn. So she wrapped the baby with cloths and laid him in a box where animals are fed.—Luke 2:6, 7

Object Needed: Picture of an inn full of people or a door with a "No Vacancy" sign on it.

"Good *morning!" (You.)*

"Good morning!" *(Their response.)*

"This morning I have a picture for you *(Hold up picture for all the children to see.)* to look at. This is a picture of an inn *(Or, "the door of an inn.")*, which is like a hotel or motel in Bible times. As you can see, it's full of people. So full *(Point to picture for emphasis.*), in fact, there's no room for anyone else inside.

(Lay picture face up in your lap as that thought sinks in. Then resume speaking.) "That's what happened when Jesus was born, wasn't it? The Bible tells us *(Look around at the children.)* in Luke 2:6 and 7 that 'While Joseph and Mary were in Bethlehem, the time came for her to have the baby. She gave birth to her first son. There were no rooms left in the inn. So she wrapped the baby with cloths and laid him in a box where animals are fed.' Imagine a place being so full there was *no room for Jesus!*

"Well, what about *(Point with index finger.)* your heart? Is there *(Look around at children as you talk.)* room in your heart for Jesus? Or is it full of too much other stuff? *(Point with index finger for emphasis.)* Now, we need *some* other things in our hearts, just as the inn needed some of those other people. For example, we need love in our hearts for our *(Count off on fingers.)* parents, and for our brothers and sisters, and for our friends, and for all living creatures. But what happens when we begin to love money, and all the things money can buy, and having a good time all the time? *(You don't want a verbal response here; you just want to make them think—so keep moving!)* Well, our *(Tap on your heart.)* hearts become so full of other things, there's no room for Jesus!

(Smile!) "So we need *(Point index finger for emphasis as you look around at the children.)* to *make* room in our hearts for Jesus. We need to use some time every day to talk to Jesus in prayer and to listen to the Bible being read to us so we can get to know Jesus. So he can make us sorry for our sins. So we can find forgiveness and make room in our lives and hearts for Jesus!

"All right, let's bow our heads and close our eyes."

Prayer: "Dear God, thank you for loving us very, very much and being with us to help us do what is right. Please help us to pray to you and listen to the Bible so we can come to love you and make room in our hearts for you. In Jesus' name we pray. Amen."

2

Who Is Jesus?

The other followers told Thomas, "We saw the Lord." But Thomas said, "I will not believe it until I see the nail marks in his hands. And I will not believe until I put my finger where the nails were and put my hand into his side."—John 20:25

Object Needed: None. It is good, occasionally, to have nothing in your hands, for the unusual is always an attention-getter! This ploy should be used, however, only occasionally.

"Good *morning!*" (*You.*)
"Good morning!" (*Their response.*)
"This morning we're going to talk about something a little person taught (*Point to yourself.*) a big person! There's a lady who does children's sermons in her church. Whenever she does them, she wears a white choir robe. One morning when she was walking into the sanctuary (*Or "big church."*) a little boy stopped her by pulling on her robe. When she looked down to see who it was, he said, (*Make your eyes big and your voice animated.*) 'Are you—Jesus?' (*There will probably be some laughter from the adults here, so pause very briefly and then continue.*) And she thought to herself, (*Put your index finger against your chin and smile.*) 'My! That's the nicest thing anyone will ever ask me!' But (*For emphasis, point with index finger.*) she noticed the little boy didn't say, '*Aren't* you Jesus?' He said, '*Are* you Jesus?'

"So the lady asked him, 'What makes you think I might be Jesus?' And the little boy said, 'Well, I've seen pictures of him, and he always wore a robe like the one *you* wear. And he had long brown hair, like *you* have. And he had brown eyes, like *you* do. And (*Say this sentence with a big smile and much joy.*) he *loved* children, just like *you* do!'

"So the lady asked him, 'Why do you think I might *not* be Jesus?' And the little boy (*Wrinkle your brow and look very serious here.*) looked very serious and said, 'Well, I don't think Jesus paints (*Very slight pause; then say next two words with emphasis.*) his fingernails!'

(*There will be laughter here. You laugh too. Then proceed.*)
"That's a funny story! That's a cute story. (*No exclamation point after this second sentence. You are deliberately calming the children*

down.) But it made that lady think about (*Hold up three fingers for all the children to see. Always be sure to include all the children to let them know that all are welcome and included in God's house. This is a very important concept to establish and maintain whenever you give one of these talks.*) three important things. First, that little boy had really paid attention in Sunday school and children's church (*Or Vacation Bible School or "big church."*) and when his mother read to him because he had noticed and remembered a number of things about Jesus. He remembered (*Count off on fingers.*) how Jesus looks in the paintings and drawings (*Be sure to use "paintings and drawings" here to emphasize that we don't have photographs to show us exactly what Jesus looked like.*) we have of him, and he remembered what Jesus wore.

"Second, that little boy reminds me of my favorite (*Or "one of the disciples."*) disciple, Thomas. You remember (*Look around at the children.*) Thomas was the disciple who refused to believe something just because someone had *told* him it was true. No, Thomas and this little boy had the courage, the patience, and the strength to (*Speak slowly and deliberately here: this is your main point!*) find out for themselves who Jesus was. (*Emphasize by pointing with your index finger.*) You see, the most important thing God asks all of us to do with our lives is to find out for ourselves who Jesus is! Now, suppose that little boy had said, 'Well, this person looks like Jesus, and dresses like Jesus, and does one of the things Jesus does—so it must be Jesus!' He would have been very wrong! That lady wasn't Jesus!

"And the third important thing about this story is that the little boy had realized that Jesus loves children. He does—very, very much. In fact, in the Bible, in the New Testament, Jesus tells the rest of us how we are supposed to treat children. We are to love you as Jesus loves you. We are to teach you good things, and we are to protect you from bad things.

"So, when you think about all the things we've talked about today, (*Emphasize with both hands.*) I want you to remember one thing: the most important thing God asks all of us to do with our lives is to find out for ourselves who Jesus is.

"All right (*Smile.*), let's bow our heads and close our eyes."

Prayer: "Dear God, thank you for loving us so very, very much. Please help us to remember that the most important thing you ask us to do with our lives is to find out for ourselves who Jesus is! In Jesus' name we pray. Amen."

3

Strawberries or Potatoes?

Jesus answered, "I am the way. And I am the truth and the life. The only way to the Father is through me."—John 14:6

Objects Needed: (1) A recipe box or notebook or accordion file for a cookbook, and (2) a recipe for strawberry pie.

(Walk in carrying prop in your left hand, if you are right-handed. Sit down and place box, notebook, file, or book in your lap. Look around at children and smile.)

"Good *morning!*" *(You.)*
"Good morning!"*(Their response.)*
"In our talks, *(Or whatever you call them in your church.),* we have said that *(Count off on fingers.)* we have to believe that Jesus is the

Son of God. We have to be sorry for the bad things we have done. And we have to ask God to forgive us and be with us and help us to do what is right. *(Frown and furrow your brow.)* But do we really have to do all that? I mean, *(Spread your hands.)* do we really *have* to obey Jesus?*(Keep moving!)*

"Let's find out. I've brought with me this morning a recipe for something delicious. *(Open book to recipe for strawberry pie, or take card out of box, file, or notebook. Hold up for all the children to see.)* It's the recipe for strawberry pie! Yum! Boy, that's good stuff! *(Smile like you really mean it.)* It's good because *(Look at recipe.)* it has strawberries, and sugar, and whipped cream in it! Yum!

"But, *(Hold up your index finger for emphasis.)* wait a minute, do we really need all that stuff? I mean, it would be just as good if we took out the strawberries and put in potatoes, wouldn't it? *(Look at children for a few seconds. Then resume speaking. Shake your head and scrunch up your face.)* Noooooo. Potatoes and whipped cream! *(Make a face.)* No! We'd better *(Nod your head.)* put the strawberries back in. It just wouldn't be strawberry pie without the strawberries, would it?

(Again, hold up index finger for emphasis.) "Well, what about the *(Point to recipe card.)* whipped cream? We don't really *(Shake your head.)* need the cream, do we? Why don't we use chicken gravy *(Make your eyes big.)* instead? *(Let that sink in for just a few seconds. Then resume speaking. Again, make a face and shake your head.)* Nooooooo! We don't want chicken gravy in strawberry pie! We'd better *(Nod your head.)* put the whipped cream back in. It just *(Shake your head.)* wouldn't be strawberry pie without whipped cream in it!

(Put recipe back in your lap. Look more serious now.)

"Well, the same thing is true about salvation. We can't *(Look around at children. This is your key point.)* be saved without Jesus. The Bible tells us in John 14:6, 'Jesus *(Hold up index finger for emphasis.)* answered, "I am the way. And I am the truth and the life. The only way to the Father is through me."' So that answers our *(Smile.)* question, doesn't it? The *only* way *any* of us can be saved is through Jesus. We can't substitute anything or anyone else!

"All right, let's bow our heads and close our eyes."

Prayer: "Dear God, thank you for making it possible for us to be saved. Please help us to remember that we can't be saved without Jesus. In Jesus' name we pray. Amen."

4

What God Forgives

The Lord forgives people for wrong and sin and turning against him.—Exodus 34:7

Object Needed: A copy of the Bible. Be sure it is bound in such a way as to be instantly recognizable as being a Bible and not something else. For example, one bound in black leather and marked with a small satin ribbon. If possible, use the same Bible every time one is called for as a prop in these talks. The children will notice this, and it will give them the desired impression, i.e., that the Bible is a part of your life.

(To create the desired entrance, walk in with a sense of purpose, carrying the Bible in your left hand, if you are right-handed. If left-

11

handed, carry it in your right hand. Sit down and immediately begin dialogue, holding Bible on your lap. Look at the children.)

"Good *morning!" (You.)*
"Good morning!" *(Their response.)*

"In our talks the last few weeks, we've *(Look around at the children while you talk.)* learned that *(Count off on your fingers.)* the most important thing we can do with our lives is to find out for ourselves who Jesus is. We've also learned that we need to care that Jesus is the perfect Son of God, and we need to be sorry for the bad things we've done and ask God to forgive us. So that raises a very important question, doesn't it? *(No, you don't want a verbal answer here, just a mental one, so keep talking.)* We need to know, is there anything God can't forgive? *(Repeat question.)* Is there anything we can do that is so small God wouldn't care about it or anything so big God *can't* forgive it?

"No, God forgives everything as soon as a person is sorry for a sin and asks God for forgiveness. Nothing is so small that God doesn't care about it. *(Hold Bible up, in your lap, with both hands.)* The Bible says God even cares when a little bird falls out of a tree! And nothing is too big for God to forgive. *(This is a crucial point for this is something that really frightens children, i.e., the idea that they can do something so big and so awful that God can never forgive them.)* The Bible tells us that Moses, that great hero of God, was a murderer before God straightened him out. King David, who did so many wonderful things for God, at one time did a lot of bad things. And a man named Saul was really bad: he went around looking for Christians so he could have them put to death. But then he met God and became Paul, one of the greatest missionaries who ever lived.

(Lay Bible reverently back in your lap.) "So whenever you children think about forgiveness, I want you to remember that no matter what you do, if you are truly sorry later and ask God for forgiveness, he will forgive you!"

Prayer: "Dear God, thank you for forgiving us when we are sorry for the bad things we do and ask you for forgiveness. Please help us to remember that you can forgive anything we are truly sorry for. In Jesus' name we pray. Amen."

5

What Is an Ego?

Pride will destroy a person. A proud attitude leads to ruin.—
Proverbs 16:18

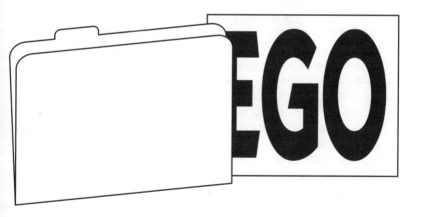

Objects Needed: (1) The word EGO printed in large block letters on
an 8 1/2 x 11 inch piece of white poster board; and (2) a file folder,
colored if possible, or a flat bag.

*(Walk in carrying poster in file folder or bag in your left hand, if you
are right-handed. Sit down and lay folder or bag in your lap.)*

"Good *morning!!*"*(You.)*

"Good morning!" *(Their response.)*

"In last week's *(Look around at children as you continue talking.)* talk, we learned that God can forgive anything we are truly sorry for. *(Make your eyes big and look excited.)* So that means there really isn't anything to keep us from going to God in prayer and asking him to forgive us and be with us to help us do what is right. *(Pause briefly and let that sink in.)*

(Frown and look confused.) "Well, then, since that's true, why do some people never ask God for forgiveness? Why do some people never *(Look around at children.)* ask Jesus to help them live the way he wants them to? *(Hold up your index finger to keep their minds from looking for answers at this point.)* Because of a tiny little word that causes great big problems. That little word is *(Slip poster out of file folder or bag and hold up for all the children to see.)* EGO.

(Make a frowny face and resume speaking. Look at poster.) "A word that little can keep someone from obeying and letting Jesus help them live for him. Yes. Because *(Point to word.)* EGO is what people think of themselves. LOVE is what we think of other people, but EGO is what we think of ourselves. *(Lay poster face down in your lap.)* And if our egos get to be too big, if we begin to think too much of ourselves, then we don't know we *need* Jesus. You see, some people have such big egos they begin to believe that *they* can do anything and that they don't need Jesus. They are filled with pride. We need to like ourselves and to be glad we are who we are, but we need to understand that no person can do everything and *all* of us need Jesus! And we need to love other people because they need Jesus, too.

"The Bible tells us in Proverbs 16:18 that 'Pride will destroy a person. A proud attitude leads to ruin.'

"So when you think about Jesus, I want you to remember that everybody needs Jesus."

Prayer: "Dear God, thank you for being with us to help us do what is right. Please help us to remember that all of us need Jesus. In Jesus' name we pray. Amen."

6

Are Christians Supposed to be Happy?

But the Spirit gives . . . joy.—Galatians 5:22

Object Needed: A picture of Jesus *smiling.* It should be large enough for all the children to see.

(For instructions, see talk #6.)

"Good *morning!"(You.)*
"Good morning!" *(Their response.)*
"The last few weeks, we've been talking about the most wonderful person who ever lived: Jesus! So this morning I brought *(Take pic-*

ture out of folder or bag as you talk.) a picture *(Hold up for all the children to see.)* of Jesus for us to look at. Now, I'm going to ask you a question, and if you know the answer, I want you to raise your hand. *(You look at picture, too.)* What is Jesus doing?

(Ignore anyone who tries to answer without raising his or her hand. Call on the first child who raises his or her hand. Call by name, if possible. If this child gives an incorrect answer, say, "That's a good answer, but that's not what I'm looking for." Or, if he or she names something else Jesus is doing in the picture, say, "That's right; Jesus is talking to little children" or whatever, "but that's not what I'm looking for." Then go on to next raised hand. If no one gives the correct answer, then give it yourself, and move on. You don't ever want to make any child feel bad or embarrassed! If some child does get it right, say, "That's RIGHT! Jesus is smiling!")

"Jesus is smiling! Now, we know that people smile when they're happy. So, if *(Look at, and point to, picture.)* Jesus is smiling *(Look at children.)*, that means he's happy. And if Jesus is happy, then that means it's all right for Christians to be happy, doesn't it? *(You do not want a verbal answer here, so keep moving.)*

(Look back at picture.) "Well, this is only a painting of Jesus. It's not a photograph, so this picture doesn't prove that Jesus ever smiled. So this picture doesn't prove that it's all right for Christians to be happy.

(Lay picture face up in your lap as you continue talking: you don't want the children to dwell on the "unhappy" part.) "But *(Smile! And look at children.)* the Bible does! The Bible tells us in *(Count off on fingers.)* Proverbs and John and Acts and Romans and Galatians and 1 Peter that Christians are supposed to be happy. Galatians 5:22 says, 'the Spirit gives . . . joy!' When you become *(Emphasize by pointing index finger.)* a Christian, the Holy Spirit fills you with joy so you will be happy. So Christians *are* supposed to be *happy*.

(Hold up picture again as you continue talking.) So although this *(Look at briefly, and point to, picture.)* is only a painting and not a photograph, we know it's true: Jesus did smile because Jesus was happy!" *(Lay picture face down in your lap.)*

Prayer: "Dear God, thank you for making it possible for people to be happy. Please help us to remember that you will be with us to help us do what is right. Then we can be happy, too. In Jesus' name we pray. Amen."

7

Is It All Right for Christians to Cry?

Jesus cried.—John 11:35

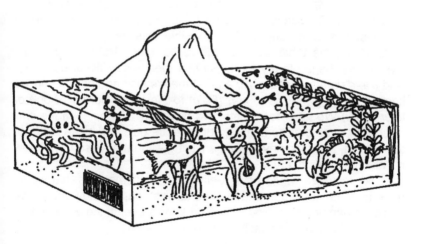

Object Needed: A box of facial tissues. It should be open, and one of the boxes designed especially for children, if possible.

(Walk in carrying the box of tissues in your left hand, if you're right-handed. Sit down and stand the box in your lap. Look at the children.)

"Good *morning!"(You.*).

"Good morning!" *(Their response.)*

"This morning I've brought something *(Hold up box of tissues for all the children to see as you continue talking.)* for you to look at that all of us see at home. It's a box of tissues. *(Stand box in your lap and hold with both hands for the next few sentences.)* When we think of tissues, we think about different things. We think about *(Talk as if you have a cold.)* having a code in our nodes! *(Resume normal speech.)* Or we think about *(Roll your eyes to the top of your head.)* cleaning up a mess *(Smile.)* we've made. Or we think about crying.

(Raise your eyebrows and look surprised.) "Crying? Are we supposed to cry? *(You don't want a verbal answer here, so keep moving.)* I mean *(Spread your hands out for emphasis and shrug your shoulders.)*, haven't you heard people say, 'Now, don't cry!' Or 'Big boys don't cry!' And in our last talk we learned that Christians are supposed to be happy! So does that mean Christians are never supposed to cry?

(Hold up index finger for emphasis and smile.) "No! The Bible tells us it's OK for Christians to cry. As Christians, we are supposed to be like Jesus. And in John 11:35, the Bible tells us, 'Jesus cried.' In Luke 19:41, the Bible says, 'Jesus came near Jerusalem. He saw the city and began to cry for it.' So that means it's OK for us to cry. And *(Hold up finger and smile again.)* there's also another reason we know it's all right for us to cry. *(Point to the inside corner of one of your eyes.)* We have tear ducts. We have tiny little holes in the corner of our eyes that do nothing but let tears out. And since God put them there, and God never does anything without a reason, we know it's all right for us to cry.

"God knew we would have feelings inside sometimes that would need to come out. So he made tears to wash our feelings out, so we could be happy again. You see, God knows everything we will ever need, and he makes it possible for us to have it!"

Prayer: "Dear God, thank you for meeting all our needs. Please help us to remember that when we have feelings that need to come out, it's OK for us to cry. In Jesus' name we pray. Amen."

8

Why We Need to Pray

Never stop praying.—1 Thessalonians 5:17

Objects Needed: (1) A portable radio and (2) the batteries that power it. The radio should be set on a suitable station, a Christian one, if possible.

(Walk in carrying radio in your left hand, if you're right-handed, and the batteries in your pocket. Sit down and place radio in upright position in your lap. The batteries should be out of sight.)

"Good *morning!" (You.)*
"Good morning!" *(Their response.)*
"This morning *(Look at radio.)* I've brought a radio for you to see.

Boy, that's nice, isn't it? I *like* radios. They play pretty music for me, and they teach me things, and they help me keep up with the weather, and they tell me the news. *(Lay index finger on chin.)* You know, there's probably something nice on the radio right now. *(Smile.)* Let's turn it on and see!

(Attempt to turn on radio. Frown. Try several times. Turn radio toward you and look perplexed.) "It doesn't work! This *is* a radio, and I did try to make it work, but it won't work! *(Raise your head, smile, and close your eyes as if you've just remembered something.)* There are no batteries in it! That's why it won't work! *(Pull batteries out of your pocket.)* So let's put some batteries in it. *(Put batteries in.)* Now let's try it. *(Turn radio on, loud enough for children to hear, but not overly loud. This is church and the atmosphere should be kept respectful.)* There! Now it works. (Turn radio off.) *It wouldn't work before because* (Speak slowly and distinctly here for you are about to make your main point.) it wasn't in touch with its power source. It won't work if it's not in touch with its power source.

(Lay radio down in your lap. You want the children at this point to pay attention to YOU.) "Did you know the same thing is true of people? That's right. People won't work if they're not in touch with their power source. And a person's power source is God. *(Repeat.)* The way we get in touch with God is through prayer. And we have to do it every day. *(Tap your radio with your finger a moment.)* We're just like this radio. It has to be in touch with its power source every day in order to work. We have to be in touch with God every day in order to work. The Bible tells us in 1 Thessalonians 5:17 that we are to 'never stop praying.' We are to 'never stop praying.' That means that anytime we are awake, we need to be aware of God's presence and to talk to him about all of our feelings and decisions. We need to always be in touch with God.

"The Bible also gives us many examples of how often Jesus prayed. And if *Jesus* needed to pray, *we* certainly do!

(Take batteries out of radio and hold up for the children to see.) "So whenever you hear a radio, I want you to remember that Christians need to pray every day."

Prayer: "Dear God, thank you for always being there for us. Please help us to remember to pray to you every day. In Jesus' name we pray. Amen."

9

What Happens When We Pray?

You, Lord, give true peace. You give peace to those who depend on you. You give peace to those who trust you.—Isaiah 26:3

Object Needed: A picture of a person who is obviously very worried. It should be big enough for all the children to see and easily comprehend.

(For instructions, see talk #6.)

"Good *morning!" (You.)*

"Good morning!" *(Their response.)*

"In our last talk we saw how important *(Look around at the children while you talk.)* it is for Christians to pray. We learned that when we talk to God, we are in touch with our power source. But what *happens* when we get in touch with our power source? What *happens* when we talk to God? *(You do not want a verbal response here—so keep moving!)*

"It keeps us—from worrying! *(Smile.)* Yes, praying keeps us from worrying. Now, when we worry, we look funny. We *(Take picture out of folder or bag as you talk and hold it up for all the children to see.)* look like this when we worry! *(Wrinkle up your nose.)* Now, that's no fun, *(Shake your head.)* is it? We don't want to worry. It makes us look funny, and the Bible says worrying is a sin. *(Nod your head.)* Yes, the Bible says worrying is a sin. *(Lay picture facedown in your lap as you continue talking.)* You see, in Philippians 4:19, the Bible says, 'God will use his riches in Christ Jesus to give you everything you need.' *(Repeat verse.)* Wow! That's wonderful! God has promised to *give us everything* we need. So, if we worry, we are saying we don't trust God to keep his word. *(Repeat from "if.")* God *always* keeps his word—so worrying is a sin.

"Instead of worrying, we should pray. In Psalm 55:22, the Bible says, 'Give your worries to the Lord.' And, then, while God is busy taking care of our needs, he will fill us with peace! *(Repeat from "while.")* In Isaiah 26:3, the Bible says, 'You, Lord, give true peace. You give peace to those who depend on you. You give peace to those who trust you.'

"So, the next time you feel like worrying about something, remember: no matter what it is, pray about it. Ask God to take care of it for you. And he will!"

Prayer: "Dear God, thank you for promising to meet all of our needs. Please help us to remember that worrying is a sin and that we should ask you to take care of us. In Jesus' name we pray. Amen."

How Should We Pray?

So when you pray, you should pray like this: "Our Father in heaven, we pray that your name will always be kept holy. We pray that your kingdom will come. We pray that what you want will be done, here on earth as it is in heaven. Give us the food we need for each day. Forgive the sins we have done, just as we have forgiven those who did wrong to us. Do not cause us to be tested; but save us from the Evil One."— Matthew 6:9-13

The LORD'S PRAYER

Our Father
which art in heaven,
Hallowed be thy name.
Thy kingdom come.
Thy will be done
in earth, as it is in heaven.
Give us this day
our daily bread.
And forgive us our debts,
as we forgive our debtors.
And lead us not
into temptation,
but deliver us from evil:
for thine is the kingdom,
and the power,
and the glory, for ever
          Amen.

Object Needed: A card or bookmark or some other item bearing a copy of the Lord's Prayer on it. Size here is not important.

(For instructions, see talk #6.)

"Good *morning*!" *(You.)*
"Good morning!" *(Their response.)*
"In our last two talks, we talked about why Christians should pray and what happens when we pray. But today *(Hold up index finger and smile!)* we are going to talk about *how* to pray. *(Look around at the children as you continue talking—and do just that: continue talking. As you raise issues, you only want mental responses, so keep*

talking.) Now, that's important *(Nod your head.)*, isn't it? I mean, if we're going to pray, we want to do it right!

"Well, the Bible gives us directions on how to pray. That's right. God always gives us directions on how to do what we need to do. We are told how to pray in Matthew 6:9-13 and in John 14:14. These verses in Matthew are frequently called *(Take card or whatever out of folder or bag as you talk and hold it up for all the children to see.)* the Lord's Prayer and we see copies of it on cards and bookmarks and other pretty things. *(Turn card or whatever in your direction now and look at it with a slight frown.)* Now, does that mean we are supposed to say *(Point to words on cards.)* these same *words* every time we pray? *(Shake your head.)* Nooooo! *(Look up and smile.)* The Lord's Prayer tells us *how* to pray, *not* what to say. *(Lay card face up in your lap as you continue talking.)* These verses from Matthew tell us that when we pray, about anything, we should call God by name. We should call God by name. That shows that we're talking to *him* and that we *know* who he is! So we should call God by name when we pray.

"These verses tells us next that when we pray, we should ask for whatever *we* think we need, and then ask God to do whatever *he* knows is best. *(Repeat from first "we.")* Since the whole point of praying to God is to have him take care of us, then we want to be sure to let him do what he knows is best!

"Whenever I do one of these talks for you, I always say a prayer at the end, and I always say, 'In Jesus' name.' Why do I do that? Because *(Emphasize by pointing with index finger.)* in John 14:14, Jesus says, 'If you ask me for anything in my name, I will do it.' So whenever we pray, we should remember to *(Count off on your fingers.)* call God by name: you can call him 'Dear God' or 'Heavenly Father' or whatever you like to call him. Just be yourself! Number two, we are to ask for whatever we think we need, and then ask God to do whatever he knows is best. And, third, we are to end our prayer by saying, 'In Jesus' name.' That means you're not being selfish: you're praying because you know it makes Jesus *happy* for you to pray!"

Prayer: "Dear God, thank you for teaching us how to pray. Please help us to remember to call you by name, to ask for whatever we think we need and then ask you to do whatever you know is best, and then to ask for these things in Jesus' name. For this we pray in Jesus' name. Amen."

24

11

When Jesus Plants a Garden

Do not change yourselves to be like the people of this world. But be changed within by a new way of thinking. Then you will be able to decide what God wants for you. And you will be able to know what is good and pleasing to God and what is perfect.—Romans 12:2

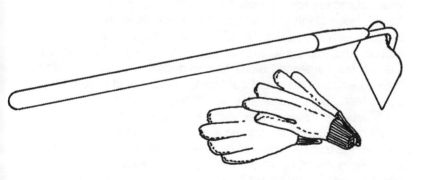

Objects Needed: (1) A garden hoe, preferably a child's small one, as it will be easier to handle, and (2) a pair of gardening gloves.

(Walk in carrying hoe and gloves in one hand. Sit down and put gloves in your lap and lay hoe beside you.)

"Good *morning!" (You*.)

"Good morning!" (*Their response*.)

"This morning we're going to talk about (*Look around at children and smile*.) something fun that happens in the spring. (*Or "summer" if that's more accurate for your part of the country*.) We're going to talk about making a garden.

"Now, the first thing we do when we make a garden is (*Put on gardening gloves as you continue to talk*.) put on our gloves so we won't hurt our hands. But the second thing we do is (*Pick up hoe and hold in both hands as if you are about to chop weeds*.) get the ground ready for good things to grow. And to do that, we have to (*Make very gentle chopping motions with your hoe, being very careful NOT to hit one of the children*.) get rid of the weeds. We have to get rid of the weeds, because, if we don't, the weeds will take up all the ground and there won't be room left over for *good* things to grow. (*Repeat from "if."*) (*Put hoe on floor beside you, but gloves stay on*.)

(*Look around at children*.) "Well, you know something, Boys and Girls? That's exactly what Jesus does when *he* plants a garden! When Jesus plants a garden, he has to get the weeds out first. And you know (*Smile*.) where Jesus plants his gardens? (*You don't want a verbal answer here, so keep moving*.) In our hearts! (*Point to your heart*.) Jesus plants his gardens in people's heart. Jesus plants *good* things in people's hearts. He (*Count off on fingers*.) plants hope, and peace, and love, and the answers to our questions about life. (*Repeat last sentence*.) But before he does that (*Look around at children*.), he has to get out of our hearts the weeds of (*Count off on fingers*.) fear, and sadness, and ugly thoughts. Jesus has to get out of our hearts the weeds of fear, and sadness, and ugly thoughts.

(*Fold your hands in your lap and look at children*.) "But Jesus will only get the bad things out of our hearts if we *let* him! Jesus *wants* to put really good things in our hearts, but we have to be willing to let him take the bad things out."

Prayer: "Dear God, thank you for wanting to put hope, and peace, and love, and the answers to our questions about life in our hearts. Please help us to remember that before you will do that, we will have to give you our fear, and our sadness, and our ugly thoughts. In Jesus' name we pay. Amen."

12

Where the Answers Are

But the wisdom that comes from God is like this: First, it is pure. Then it is also peaceful, gentle, and easy to please. This wisdom is always ready to help those who are troubled and to do good for others. This wisdom is always fair and honest.—James 3:17

Object Needed: A potted plant that follows the direction of the sun as it grows.

(*Walk in carrying plant in one hand. Sit down and balance pot in your lap using both hands.*)

"Good *morning!*" (*You.*)
"Good morning!" (*Their response.*)

"This morning I've brought a little green plant (*Hold up for all the children to see.*) for you to see. It's called (*Give name of particular species.*) and it lives on my windowsill. (*Or "balcony," or "porch," or "in my neighbor's window," or whatever.*) I like this little plant because it's pretty. But it also has a funny (*Look around at children as you talk.*) little habit. It likes to follow the sun. Every day when I come home from work, it has turned itself (*Turn plant.*) to face the sun. So every day I turn it back around to face me. (*Or my neighbor turns it back to face inside his house.*) And the next day, it turns toward the sun again!

(*Holding the plant with one hand, put other hand on hip and look perplexed.*) "What a funny thing for a plant to do! Why doesn't it just sit still in its little pot?" (*At this point, you may get some unsolicited answers. If you do, that's OK. Normally, it's much better for them to raise their hands before they speak, but since this is not a direct question, wait until someone speaks out before you follow the directions in talk #9.*)

"The plant turns because it wants to follow the sun. (*Repeat.*) And it wants to do that because it knows that the secret of how plants live comes from—the sun.

(*Rest pot on your lap and look at children.*) "Well, the same thing is true of people and the Son of God. Just as the secret of how plants live comes from the sun in the sky, so the secret of how people live comes from Jesus, the Son of God. If we want to be (*Tap the side of your head.*) smart and successful, if we want to really live, we need to turn and follow Jesus. (*Repeat slowly and with meaning.*) You see, the Bible says the wisdom that comes from Jesus is real. It's true.

"So the next time you see a little green plant, I want you to remember that the way to be smart and successful, the way to really live, is to follow Jesus."

Prayer: "Dear God, thank you for having all the answers. Please help us to remember to turn to you with all our questions. In Jesus' name we pray. Amen."

13

What Mothers Do

(NOTE: This talk could be used on Mother's Day.)

Look at the birds in the air. They don't plant or harvest or store food in barns. But your heavenly Father feeds the birds. And you know that you are worth much more than the birds.—Matthew 6:26

Object Needed: Mother's Day card.

(For instructions, see talk # 6.)

"Good *morning!*" (*You.*)

"Good morning!" (*Their response.*)

"I've brought something pretty for you to see this morning. (*Hold up card for all the children to see.*) It's a Mother's Day card. This card reminds us that mothers are so important a whole day is set aside for them every year!

(*Put index finger on chin as though you are trying to figure something out.*) "Well, I got to thinking about that. And (*Put card facedown in your lap as you continue to talk.*) I realized there are three (*Hold up three fingers.*) reasons why mothers are so important. There are three reasons why God made mothers.

(*Count off on fingers.*) "First of all, mothers think we're special just the way we are. (*Repeat from "mothers."*) Second, mothers feed us. (*Repeat from "mothers."*) And, third, mothers comfort us. Mothers help us feel better when things hurt us.

(*Look around at the children as you say this next, important part.*) "You know something, Boys and Girls? When we become Christians, God will do for us those three things mothers did for us as children. (*Repeat from "God."*) God (*Count off on fingers.*) thinks Christians are special just the way they are. (*Repeat.*) And God feeds us. God provides our food for us. The Bible says in Matthew 6:26, 'Look at the birds in the air. They don't plant or harvest or store food in barns. But your heavenly Father feeds the birds. And you know that you are worth much more than the birds.' And, God comforts us. God sends the Holy Spirit to help us feel better when things hurt us.

(*Smile!*) "So God gives us mothers to show us what *he* is like when we become Christians! Mothers are supposed to remind us of what *God* is like when we become Christians! (*Be a little less exuberant here; you're about to deal with a very painful subject.*) Now, some children have lost their mothers. But they can learn these things about God from whoever is serving as a mother to them."

Prayer: "Dear God, thank you for giving children mothers to love them just the way they are, to feed them, and to help them feel better when things hurt them. Please help us to remember that when we become Christians, you will do those things for us. In Jesus' name we pray. Amen."

14

What Fathers Do

(NOTE: This talk could be used on Father's Day.)

My God is very rich with the glory of Christ Jesus. God will use his riches in Christ Jesus to give you everything you need.—Philippians 4:19

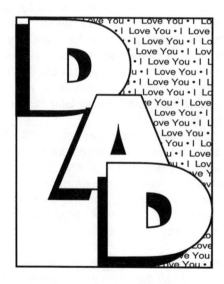

Object Needed: Father's Day card.

(For instructions, see talk #6.)

"Good *morning!"* (*You.*)

"Good morning!" (*Their response.*)

"I've brought something interesting for you to see this morning. (*Hold up card for all the children to see.*) It's a Father's Day card. This card reminds us that fathers are so important a whole day is set aside for them every year!

(*Put index finger on chin as though you are trying to figure something out.*) I thought about that and (*Put card facedown in your lap as you continue to talk.*) I realized there are three (*Hold up three fingers.*) reasons why fathers are so important. There are three reasons why God made fathers.

(*Count off on fingers.*) "First of all, fathers make a living and provide for their families. (*Repeat from "fathers."*) Second, fathers protect us from things that would hurt us. (*Repeat from "fathers."*) And, third, fathers fix things for us when they're broken. (*Repeat from "fathers."*)

(*Look around at the children as you say this next, important part.*) "You know something, Boys and Girls? When we become Christians, God will do for us those three things fathers did for us as children. (*Repeat from "God."*) God (*Count off on fingers.*) provides for us whatever we need. In Philippians 4:19 the Bible says, 'My God is very rich with the glory of Christ Jesus. God will use his riches in Christ Jesus to give you everything you need.' Isn't that (*Smile!*) wonderful? (*Keep moving.*) And God protects us from the devil who would hurt us. *(Repeat from "God.")* And God fixes our hearts and our lives when they are broken.

(*Look around at all the children and smile.*) "So God gives us fathers to show us what *he* is like when we become Christians. Fathers are supposed to remind us of what *God* is like when we become Christians. (*Be a little less exuberant here; you are about to deal with a very painful subject.*) Now, some children have lost their fathers. But they can learn these things about God from whoever is serving as a father to them."

Prayer: "Dear God, thank you for giving children fathers so they can have what they need, so they can be protected from things that would hurt them, and so when things are broken, they can have someone to fix them. Please help us to remember that when we become Christians, you will do these things for us. In Jesus' name we pray. Amen."

15

What God Does All Day

The Lord has heard my cry for help. The Lord will answer my prayer.—Psalm 6:9

Object Needed: The Bible. (*For further instructions here, see talk #5.*)

"Good *morning!*" (*You.*)
"Good morning!" (*Their response.*)
"In our last two talks (*Or whatever you call them in your church.*), we've learned (*Look around at children.*) some pretty neat things about God! We've learned that (*Count off on fingers.*) when we become Christians, God thinks we are special just the way we are. And God provides our food for us. And God sends the Holy Spirit to help us feel better when things hurt us. And God gives us what we need. And God protects us from the devil. And God fixes our hearts and our lives when they are broken.

(*Wipe your brow.*) "Phew! That's a lot (*Look around at children.*) to do! But I got to thinking about that, and I realized that's not (*Make your eyes big.*) *all* he does. There are a number of other things God does all day, but (*Hold up index finger for emphasis.*) there's one that's especially important to (*Use sweeping motion of your hand to indicate all the children.*) all of us. Every day and night, God *hears*, and *answers*, prayers. (*Repeat.*) In the Bible, (*Hold up Bible briefly for all the children to see.*) in Psalm 6:9, we are told, 'The Lord has heard my cry for help. The Lord will answer my prayer.' That tells us that when we are hurt in our hearts (*Point to your heart.*) or whenever we don't know what to do, we can pray to God, and he will hear and answer our prayer! (*Smile! And repeat from "when."*)

(*Look perplexed.*) "Well, now, does that mean that we should only pray to God when we *need* something? (*You don't want a verbal answer here so keep moving.*) No. We *should always* pray to God when we need something, but the Bible (*Hold up Bible briefly for all the children to see.*) says we should *also* pray to God when we just want to tell him how much we love him! (*Repeat from "we should always."*) In Psalm 18:1, the Psalmist says, 'I love you, Lord. You are my strength.' Isn't it (*Smile like you really mean it.*) wonderful to know that we can actually talk to God?"

Prayer: "Dear God, thank you for letting us pray to you. Please help us to remember that we can talk to you anytime we need help and we can talk to you when we just want to say, 'I love you.' In Jesus' name we pray. Amen."

16

What the Holy Spirit Does

Also, the Spirit helps us. We are very weak, but the Spirit helps us with our weakness. We do not know how to pray as we should. But the Spirit himself speaks to God for us, even begs God for us. The Spirit speaks to God with deep feelings that words cannot explain.—Romans 8:26

Object Needed: The Bible. Have passages referred to in talk marked in Bible. (*For further instructions here, see talk #5.*)

"Good *morning!*" (*You.*)

"Good morning!" (*Their response.*)

"In our talks (*Or whatever you call them in your church.*) lately, we've learned a little bit (*Look around at children.*) about the Holy Spirit. We've learned that when things hurt us, God sends the Holy Spirit to help us feel better. (*Smile.*) That's a neat thought, isn't it? When we hurt, God cares—and sends the Holy Spirit to help us feel better!

(*Hold up index finger for emphasis.*) "But the Bible tells us the Holy Spirit *also* does some other very special things for Christians. (*Open Bible to first marker as you continue talking.*) In Romans 8:26, the Bible says, 'Also, the Spirit *helps* us. We are very weak, but the Spirit *helps* us with our weakness.' And in (*Turn to second marked passage.*) John 14:16, Jesus said, 'I will ask the Father, and he will give you another Helper. He will give you this Helper to be with you forever.' (*Smile!*) Wow! Isn't that wonderful? When we want to do what is right, but we just can't (*Frown and shake your head.*) do it all by ourselves, if we ask God for help, he will send the Holy Spirit to help us!

(*Turn to third marked passage as you continue talking.*) "And, in John 14:26, Jesus said, 'The Helper will teach you everything. He will cause you to remember all the things I told you. This Helper is the Holy Spirit whom the Father will send in my name.' This means when we read the Bible and try to understand it, the Holy Spirit helps us. The Holy Spirit helps us learn how to be good!"

Prayer: "Dear God, thank you for giving us the Holy Spirit. Please help us to remember that when we hurt, we should tell you about it; when we need help being good, we should ask you for help; and when we want to understand the Bible, we should ask you to help us—so you can send the Holy Spirit to do all these things for us! In Jesus' name we pray. Amen."

17

Why God Lets People Talk

So go and make followers of all people in the world. Baptize them in the name of the Father and the Son and the Holy Spirit. Teach them to obey everything that I have told you. You can be sure that I will be with you always. I will continue with you until the end of the world.—Matthew 28:19, 20

Object Needed: Picture in a book or on a card of Jesus preaching. It should be large enough for all the children to see and recognize. (*For further instructions here, see talk #6.*)

"Good *morning!*" (*You.*)

"Good morning!" (*Their response.*)

"This morning we're going to talk about—talking! Now, people are the only creatures who can talk, aren't they? (*Nod your head.*) Yes. God made lots of live creatures, (*Count off on fingers*) all kinds of animals and people. But people are the only ones who can *talk*.

(*Look perplexed.*) "Well, if it isn't important for all those other creatures to talk, why on earth did God make it possible for *people* to talk? (*Keep moving.*) God lets (*Smile.*) people talk because he wants us to do (*Hold up three fingers.*) three things. (*Count off on fingers.*) First, God wants us to praise him. (*Repeat from "God."*) That means we should tell God we love him and tell him how wonderful he is. (*Repeat from "we should."*) This makes God happy—and it makes *us* feel (*Smile.*) good, too!

"Second, God wants us to pray for each other. (*Repeat from "God."*) When other people hurt or need something, we should pray for them. This makes God happy, and it helps the people we pray for. And, third, God lets people talk so we can tell each other about Jesus. (*Repeat from "God."*) When Jesus lived on earth, he did all three of these things. (*Pull picture out of folder or open book to marker. Hold up picture for all the children to see as you continue talking.*) Here we have a picture of Jesus telling other people who he was and how to be saved. And when Jesus got ready to go back to Heaven, he said for *us* to do all these things. When we tell other people about Jesus, it makes God happy and it helps other people get to Heaven.

(*Put picture face up in your lap.*) "Isn't that exciting? (*Smile and look around at the children.*) We're not supposed (*Shake your head.*) to use our voices to tell lies or say ugly things or hurt people. We're supposed to use our voices the way *Jesus* did!

Prayer: "Dear God, thank you for letting us talk. Please help us remember to use our voices as Jesus did: to praise you, to pray for each other, and to tell people about Jesus. In Jesus' name we pray. Amen."

18

What God Thinks of Me

For God loved the world so much that he gave his only Son. God gave his Son so that whoever believes in him may not be lost, but have eternal life.—John 3:16

Objects Needed: (1) Three greeting cards you or a friend have received or you have bought to send to someone, that show how the sender feels about that person. (2) Your Bible. (*For further instructions here, see talks #5 and #6.*)

"Good *morning!*" (*You*.)

"Good morning!" (*Their response*.)

"Today we are going to read some cards. (*Pull out first one.*) This one says (*Read card, then hold it up briefly for all the children to see. Lay it in your lap as you continue talking. Repeat same procedure for all three cards.*) These cards (*Look around at children.*) are nice. They tell us someone cares about someone else. We all want someone to care about us. That means a lot.

"But if (*Hold up index finger for emphasis.*) it's important to us to know how other *people* feel about us, it's *really* important for us to know how *God* feels about (*Nod head.*) us! After all, (*Make your eyes big and speak very distinctly: you are about to make a big point.*) he *is* God! Wouldn't it be nice if God (*Smile.*) sent each of us a card to tell us how he feels about us? Well, Boys and Girls: he did! (*Hold up Bible for all the children to see.*) It's called the Bible. The Bible is a personal message to *each* of us from God, telling us how he feels about us. The whole Bible does this, but the verse that says it best is John 3:16. (*Open Bible and read Scripture, slowly and with emphasis and with a joyful expression on your face: you are telling these children the most wonderful thing on earth.*) 'For God loved the world *so much* that he gave his only Son. God gave his Son so that whoever believes in him may not be lost, but have eternal life.' God loves *each* one of you so much, he sent his son Jesus to die for our sins so all of us can go to Heaven. Now THAT'S LOVE!

"So the next time you wonder whether anybody cares about you, remember that God does. Remember that (*Close Bible and hold up for the children to see.*) the whole Bible was written by God to tell us how *much* God loves *each* one of us!"

Prayer: (*Lay Bible reverently in your lap.*) "Dear God, thank you for giving us the Bible. Please help us to remember that the Bible is a personal message to each one of us telling us how *much* you love us. In Jesus' name we pray. Amen."

19

The Soul Doctor

The Son of Man came to find lost people and save them.—Luke 19:10

Objects Needed: A medical doctor and a member of the teaching profession (i.e. a teacher, a school principal, or a superintendent of education) you've alerted in advance. Ideally, these individuals will be members of your church, but wherever they're from, they should be Christian people you would feel good about holding up as examples for the children in your church. These individuals should sit in the congregation until you summon them.

"Good *morning!" (You*.)

"Good morning!" (*Their response*.)

"This morning I've asked two friends of ours to help us with our talk. (*Or whatever you call them in your church*.) (*Look up at congregation*.) Will Dr. (*Call name of medical doctor*.) and (*Call name of other "prop."*) please come forward. (*Keep eyes on the two props as they come forward to encourage the children to do so. You want to be sure to hold the children's attention while you're not talking to them*.) Thank you. I need you two to stand right here (*Motion to desired spots*.) so all the children can see you. Thank you.

(*Look back at children, and then at prop, as long as the props are standing there. Point to medical doctor*.) "This is Dr. _____ . She (*Or he*.) is a medical doctor. That means she takes care of our bodies (*Touch your own shoulder*.) for us. Sometimes our bodies get hurt or sick and doctors like Dr. _____ save our bodies and make them what God meant for them to be. (*Point to second prop*.) And this is Dr. _____ . He is a different kind of doctor. He is (*Give title*.). That means he takes care of our minds (*Touch your own head*.) for us. He helps us save our minds and make them what God meant for them to be.

(*Dismiss your props.*) "Thank you very much!"

(*Look back at children and count off on fingers.*) "Now, that takes care of our bodies and our minds. But what about our souls? All of us have souls. And they're very important because our souls live forever and ever and ever and ever! And our souls get sick and messed up too. (*Smile, and point index finger for emphasis.*) Well, God thought of that, too. You see, God thinks of everything we will ever need. God has a doctor for our souls, too. His name is Jesus. God knew all of us would let sin mess up our souls and make them sick, so he sent Jesus to earth to take care of our souls. Jesus died for our sins so he could save our souls and make them what God meant for them to be."

Prayer: "Dear God, thank you for sending Jesus to save our souls. Please help us to remember that you will be with us and help us to do what is right. In Jesus' name we pray. Amen."

20

What the Bible Doesn't Do

There are many other things that Jesus did. If every one of them were written down, I think the whole world would not be big enough for all the books that would be written.—John 21:25

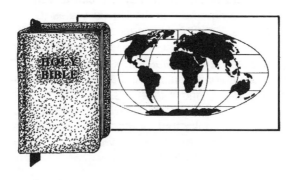

Objects Needed: (1) A map of the world. It should be big enough for the children to recognize what it is. (2) Your Bible. (*For further instructions here, see talks #5 and #6.*)

"Good *morning!*" (*You.*)

"Good morning!" (*Their response.*)

(*Hold up Bible for all the children to see.*) "We've been learning some really interesting things about (*Look around at the children as you talk.*) the Bible in our talks (*Or whatever they are called in your church.*) lately. We've learned that God himself wrote the Bible and that it's a personal message to each one of us about how much God loves us. He loves us so much he's given us Jesus to save our souls! And we know that (*Lay Bible reverently in your lap as you continue talking.*) the Bible tells us all kinds of wonderful things about Jesus. *Lots* of things. (*Count off on your fingers.*) It tells us about some of the miracles he did and about his preaching and about some of the things he said and about his family and his friends. (*Throw open your hands.*) It tells us *LOTS* of stuff about Jesus.

(*Smile, and be less exuberant now. You want them to think.*) "But you know something, Boys and Girls? There's something the Bible *doesn't* do. (*Point index finger for emphasis.*) In John 21:25, the apostle John says, 'There are many other things that Jesus did. If every one of them were written down, I think the whole world would not be big enough for all the books that would be written.' (*Make your eyes really big, put your hands in your lap, and look around at all the children.*) WOW!! 'The whole world would not be big enough for all the books that would be written' about the things Jesus did for us here on earth! The whole *world!* But 'the whole world' is sooooo *big!* (*Begin taking map out of folder or bag. Unfold as you continue talking.*) I have a picture of the world right here. (*Hold up for all the children to see.*) See? This is a map of the whole world. (*Point to your country.*) And this tiny little space right here is the United States (*Or wherever you are.*) where we live. So if this little space is the United States (*Sweep one hand across map.*), then the whole world is really, really big!

(*Fold up map and lay in your lap. This would give the children time to think about what you've said.*) "And Jesus did so many wonderful things (*Say this slowly and with awe since it's a concept you want them to be amazed by.*) that even the whole world is probably not big enough to hold the books that would tell us about Jesus! (*Shake your head back and forth briefly before you resume speaking.*) Jesus is (*Smile!*) really WONDERFUL!"

Prayer: "Dear God, thank you for being so wonderful. Please help us to remember that the Bible tells us everything we *need* to know to be saved. In Jesus' name we pray. Amen."

21

Where Lies Come From

Don't use your mouth to tell lies. Don't ever say things that are not true.—Proverbs 4:24

Object Needed: Your Bible. (*For further instructions here, see talk #5.*)

"Good *morning!*" (*You.*)
"Good morning!" (*Their response.*)
"In one of our little talks (*Or whatever they are called in your church.*) recently, we learned that we are not supposed to use our voices to tell lies. (*That was talk #20.*) And (*Hold up Bible for all the children to see.*) the Bible tells us this. (*Open to marked passage as you continue speaking.*) In Proverbs 4:24, we are told, 'Don't use your mouth to tell lies. Don't ever say things that are not true.' (*Close Bible. Then resume speaking. This momentary pause will give the children just enough time to think without getting restless!*) This is very important because Christians are supposed to be like Jesus. And Jesus (*Shake your head.*) never lies. Jesus never lies.

(*Look perplexed for a moment.*) Well, then, if Jesus always tells the truth, why are there lies in the world and *where* did they come from? (*Keep moving! Hold up index finger to signal the children that you have something more to say.*) Well, lies come from the devil because the devil is the exact opposite of God. Jesus said in (*Hold up Bible briefly.*) John 14:6 that he, Jesus, *is* the truth! So that means the devil is a lie. Everything about Jesus is real and true. Everything about the devil is false and a lie. Jesus *always* tells us the truth because he wants to *help* us. The devil *always* lies because *he* wants to *hurt* us. (*Repeat last sentence.*)

(*Make your eyes big and look at the children for a minute as if you've just thought of something important.*) "Does that mean (*Spread your hands.*) that whenever a *person* tells a lie, it *hurts* someone? (*Nod your head and continue speaking.*) Yes! That's exactly what it means! (*Use index finger again for emphasis.*) Every time anybody tells a lie, it hurts at least (*Hold up three fingers.*) three people. (*Repeat.*) It hurts (*Count off on fingers.*) the person who tells the lie because it makes them more like the devil; it hurts the person the lie is told to because it gives them the wrong information; and it hurts Jesus because he wants us to always tell the truth.

"So the next time you think you want to tell (*Nod your head, scrunch up your eyes, and smile.*) a lie, remember: lying makes us more like the devil and less like Jesus."

Prayer: "Dear God, thank you for always telling us the truth. Please help us to remember that lying makes us more like the devil and less like you. In Jesus' name we pray. Amen."

22

Why Jesus Was a Carpenter

He is ...the carpenter.—Mark 6:3

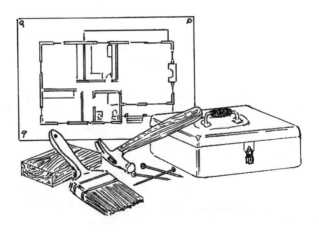

Object Needed: (1) An architect's drawing of something to be built i.e., a floor plan for a house or directions for a piece of furniture etc. (*But not a blueprint: they are too cumbersome and would take up more time than should be allotted to an object that is only a small part of this talk*.); (2) a hammer; (3) a few nails; (4) a small piece of builder's wood; (5) a paintbrush; and (6) a small toolbox to hold props 1-5.

(*Walk in carrying toolbox in your left hand, if you're right-handed. Sit down and put box on your lap.*)

"Good *morning!*" (*You*.)
"Good morning!" (*Their response.*)
"I've brought some fun things for us to look at this morning. I've brought (*Pat toolbox.*) a carpenter's toolbox with things to build stuff (*Yes, "stuff." It's a word children are very comfortable with and we only want to make quick images here; we are not making points.*) in it! (T*ake out plan and hold up for children to see as you continue speaking. Hold it up just long enough for them to be sure what it looks like.*) First, here's what the carpenter looks at to see what he's supposed to make. It's called a plan. (*Replace in box. Pick up next object briefly as you continue speaking and then replace it. Do this with all your props.*) And this is a hammer, and this is a paintbrush. These are tools the carpenter uses to build stuff. And here is a nail, and here is a piece of wood. These are some of the things a carpenter uses to build stuff.

(*Now that everything is back in your box, pause and smile, so you'll have their undivided attention.*) "When Jesus grew to be a man here on earth, we know that he didn't start off by preaching and healing people and working miracles. (*Shake your head.*) No. Jesus started off by being—a carpenter! Since God can do anything he wants to, he could have made Jesus anything. But (*Point index finger for emphasis.*) he made Jesus—a carpenter. And God always has a reason for everything he does. And there are a number of reasons why it was a good idea for Jesus to be a carpenter first. But there is (*Hold up one finger.*) one very important reason why he was a carpenter. We learned in one of our other talks (*Or whatever they are called in your church.*) that Jesus came to earth to save our souls and make them what God meant for them to be. (*That was talk #20.*) In other words, when we let Jesus come into our hearts, he (*Pat toolbox.*) *builds* our lives according to (*Hold up rolled or folded plan.*) God's plan for us. Jesus is God's carpenter who builds our lives according to God's plan for us.

45

(*Put plan back in box as you continue speaking*.) "So whenever you see a hammer or a nail, I want you to remember that when we let Jesus come into our hearts, he builds our lives according to God's plan."

Prayer: "Dear God, thank you for having a plan for our lives. Please help us to remember to let Jesus build our lives. In Jesus' name we pray. Amen."

23

What God Can't Do

Is anything too hard for the Lord? No!—Genesis 18:14

Objects Needed: A couple of members of your church who do a number of different things, either in the church or in the community. (*For further instructions here, see talk #20.*)

"Good *morning!*" (*You*.)
"Good morning!" (*Their response*.)
"Once again, I've asked some friends of ours to help us with our talk (*Or whatever they are called in your church.*) today. (*Look up at congregation or choir loft or wherever your "props" are as you summon them.*) Will Mrs. _____ and Mr. _____ please come forward and stand where the children can see you? (*Point to Mrs. _____ .*) This is Mrs. _____ . She sings in the choir. And plays the handbells. And teaches Sunday school. And directs our women's voice group. She can do *lots* of things. (*Turn to Mrs. _____ .*) Mrs. _____ , I would like for you to go over to that (*Point*.) first pew full of people (*Or, "the piano," or anything that is incredibly heavy and in full view of the children.*) and pick it up and bring it over here. (*Mrs. _____ will look at the object you've just mentioned incredulously and then at you and back at the object.*

Then she will tell you that it's impossible; she can't do what you've asked her. At this point, you should be surprised and look at her.) You can't *do* that? But you do (*Shrug shoulders and spread out your hands.*) so many things. You can't (*Repeat command.*)? (*She'll say "no." Shake your head as if you're stunned and then resume speaking.*) OK, well, (*Look at Mrs. _____ .*) thank you anyway. (*Dismiss Mrs. _____ with a wave of your hand. She should go back to her seat. Then look at children.*) She can't (*Repeat command.*).

"Well, (*Brighten.*) maybe Mr. _____ can help us. (*Point to "prop" #2.*) Mr. _____ is a banker. And he's on lots of committees downtown. And he's a deacon in our church. He can do lots of things. (*Turn to Mr. _____ .*) Mr. _____ , I would like for you to go over to the piano (*Or, "organ."*.) and sit down and play Handel's "Messiah" for us! (*NOTE: Be very sure the person you choose CANNOT, in fact, DO this! Mr. _____ , at this point, will look at you as if you've lost your mind. Then he will look at the piano or organ. And then he will look back at you and tell you what you've asked is impossible; he can't do what you've asked him to do. Again, look at him in surprise.*) You can't *do* that? But you do so many things. (*Shake your head as if you're stunned and then resume speaking.*) OK, well, (*Look at Mr. _____ .*) thank you anyway. (*Dismiss Mr. _____ with a wave of your hand. He should go back to his seat. Then look at children.*) He does so *many* things. But he can't do that. Both Mrs. _____ and Mr. _____ are smart, good people who can do lots of important things (*Smile.*), but I guess nobody can do *everything*!

(*Make your eyes big and cup your hand over your mouth. Hold this pose a moment. Then resume speaking.*) "Wait a minute! There *is* somebody who can do everything! *God* can do everything. The Bible says so. In Genesis 18:14, we see the question asked, 'Is anything too hard for the Lord? No!' (*Smile!*) There's nothing God can't do. Isn't that exciting? The heavenly Father, who takes care of (*Point to yourself.*) Christians, can do ANYTHING! There are a lot of things people can't do, but God can do anything!"

Prayer: "Dear God, thank you for being our heavenly Father. Please help us to remember that we can trust you for everything! In Jesus' name we pray. Amen."

24

The Light of the World

Later, Jesus talked to the people again. He said, "I am the light of the world. The person who follows me will never live in darkness. He will have the light that gives life."—John 8:12

Object Needed: A light in the sanctuary or room, wherever you are giving this talk.

(Walk in empty-handed and sit down. The children will be intrigued that you appear to have nothing with you. Look around at the children and smile.)

"Good *morning!" (You.)*

"Good morning!" *(Their response.)*

"Today we are going to talk about something we see every day! We are going to talk about *(Point to an overhead light in the room, if there is one. Otherwise, a lamp or whatever.) light!* We have lights (A *light.)* in here, *(Put hand back down.)* we have lights at home, we have lights in school—we have lights *(Spread your hands.)* everywhere. So lights must be *(Nod your head.)* pretty important.

(Smile.) "They are! Lights are important for *(Hold up three fingers.)* three reasons. *(Count off on fingers.)* First, light makes it possible for us to see things the way they really are. *(Repeat from "light.")* Second, light warms us. It gives off a heat that warms us. And, third, light cheers us up! When *(Point to overhead light or lamp or whatever.)* we turn the lights on, the room is more cheerful.

"Well, the very same thing is true of Jesus. The Bible tells us in John 8:12 that Jesus said, 'I am the light of the world. The person who follows me will never live in darkness. He will have the light that gives life.' When we obey Jesus, and follow him, he puts light in our hearts. And then *(Again, count off on fingers.)* we are able to see life the way it *really* is. *(Repeat from "we.")* And knowing the truth about life makes us feel warm inside. *(Repeat.)* And obeying Jesus makes us happy.*(Repeat.)*

"So whenever you see *(Point to lights or light.)* a light, I want you to remember that Jesus is the light of the world.

Prayer: "Dear God, thank you for not wanting us to live in the darkness of sin. Please help us to let you come into our lives so we can be truly happy. In Jesus' name we pray. Amen."